The *GOLF Magazine* Mental Golf Handbook

The *GOLF Magazine* Mental Golf Handbook

Gary Wiren, Ph.D.
PGA Master Professional
and the Editors of *GOLF Magazine*

The Lyons Press

First Lyons Press edition, 1999

Printed in the United States of America
Design and composition by Compset, Inc.

10 9 8 7 6 5 4 3 2 1

Library of Congress Cataloging-in-Publication Data

Wiren, Gary.
    The GOLF magazine mental golf handbook / Gary Wiren and the editors of GOLF magazine.—1st Lyons Press ed.
        p.   cm.
    ISBN 1-55821-812-2 (pbk.)
    1. Golf—Psychological aspects.   I. GOLF magazine.
    II. Title.
GV979.P75W55 1999
796.352—dc21   99-18231
                                                    CIP

Contents

Foreword

At *GOLF Magazine* we use two methods to determine the content of each issue: surveys and guts. In the survey method, questionnaires are sent to thousands of subscribers, asking—among other things—what topics they enjoy most and which kinds of articles they prefer. In the guts method, we editors simply use our intuition as kindred, hopelessly addicted golfers.

But no matter which method we use, the number one request is always for the same thing: instruction. "Give us more instruction" has been the mandate from our readers ever since the magazine began publishing, forty years ago. The reason is simple: A golfer is happiest when his game is improving.

Recently, however, we've learned a couple of things about how to present our instruction. First, you like it short and sweet. After all, most of the current population were raised on television, sound bites, and quick delivery of information—from beepers to e-mail. More than ever, we like our messages short and to the point.

And the "to the point" part is just as important as the "short" part. For the last decade or so, the most popular portion of *GOLF Magazine* has been the buff-colored section, "Private Lessons," which brings together custom-tailored instruction for five different kinds of golfers: low handicappers, high handicappers, short but straight hitters, long but crooked hitters, and senior golfers. In this way, we're able to speak more personally with our readers and help them more individually with their games.

Why am I telling you all this? Because the same kind of thinking went into the book that is now in your hands. When the people at the Lyons Press came to talk to us about a partnership in golf-book publishing, we gave them our mantra for success: instruction, succinct and focused. The result is the *GOLF Magazine* series of guides, each written concisely, edited mercilessly, and dedicated entirely to one key aspect of playing the game.

Each *GOLF Magazine* guide assembles a wealth of great advice in a package small enough to carry in your golf bag. We hope you'll use these pages to raise your game to a whole new level.

—George Peper
Editor-in-Chief
GOLF Magazine

The *GOLF Magazine* Mental Golf Handbook

Introduction

The human mind has an incredible capacity and repertoire. It can, for example, take you into the past, either recent or distant. In golf terms that means it may literally allow you to remember every shot you hit during the round just completed or leap back to shots made thirty years ago. This ability to recall can be used as a powerful asset in your game, or it can be totally ruinous. Then, within seconds your mind can transport you into an imagined future. This "yet-to-be world," totally of your own creation, also offers the same pass-or-fail double-edged sword in the arena of golf performance. Whether these mental abilities that can skip from past to future end up as your friend or enemy depends entirely upon what pictures you choose to recall.

These are but two examples of the potential of the mind; one of the most challenging elements to master in an already demanding sport. The power of the mind to influence performance should never be taken lightly. Whether you are a new golfer or one who has played for most of your life, I will guarantee you the mind plays a far greater role in your golf success than you realize.

Recognizing the tremendous value in improving one's mental strength for golf, we have produced this succinct practical treatment of the subject, a text you can cover in a short time but use for a lifetime. By working with six powerful mental traits you will be shown their importance, be given great examples of their use, and be provided with a practice tool to achieve greater strength in each area.

As you begin to read this book, let's make an assumption. You would like to play better golf and hope that what you are going to get from this material just might make that happen. Well, banish the thought immediately from your mind that it "just might." For if you honestly apply what you are about to read regarding the development of mental strength for golf, you absolutely will become a better player. In fact, the better player you become, the more important the mental aspect will be in in-

2.   During a round you putted well until the last
     hole. There, with the match on the line, plus
     a press bet, you faced a straight-in six-foot
     putt to win and left the ball dead on line for
     the center of the cup . . . but short.

The greatest scoring mistake: leaving short putts short.

3.   After hitting six perfectly straight drives on the easy opening holes, you came to the first one with a narrow fairway and promptly tightened up, slicing your drive into the trees.

Tight fairways can cause tight muscles.

4. It was your best season of playing. You had consistent scores all summer long, until the club championship, when your game fell completely apart and you made an early exit.

5. You were asked two months earlier to play in the big pro-am, but it never occurred to you that when they announced your name on the first tee your knees would be shaky and your hands trembling.

Tournament golf will add tension for the unprepared.

6. Lately when you go to play you can't seem to maintain focus on the course long enough to complete a full round with a decent score.

Some or all of these examples may be quite familiar to you. If they are, how did you react at the time? If they are not, how *would* you react? The golfer with mental strength will handle the previous scenarios

The mentally strong competitor understands there will be tough situations that must be faced.

without having them noticeably affect his or her game. Why? *Because mental strength gives you the ability to maintain composure and control in your performance while facing conditions of stress and distraction.*

Anyone who has played golf seriously will acknowledge the importance of the game's mental aspects. If that is true, then why don't we work more on improving our mental skills, giving them more attention and less lip service? I suspect that we don't because:

- Deep down we don't believe that the mental side of golf is as important as it really is.

- We only have a limited amount of practice time, which seems to be spent hitting the ball.

- We have never been properly taught how to improve the mental game through practice.

The answers to all three of these potential barriers are contained in this book. *I hope to convince you thoroughly of the value of mental strength for improving your play, show you where to find the time, and give you a program that provides sound results.*

One more observation before we start. The golfing world has been struck by "Tigermania," the unprecedented hype surrounding the new man (he's no kid) on the block, Eldridge "Tiger" Woods. Ama-

Golfers participate far more in ball-hitting practice than mental practice.

teurs and professionals alike are amazed not only by his prodigious length but also by his wonderful short game touch. But when I hear someone singing praise for his ball striking or touting his impressive stats I always interject this statement: "Are you aware that he has had a mental coach since he was eight years old!" That's right, since the age of eight. No player before in the history of the game has had thirteen years of psychological coaching prior to launching his/her career as a professional; not Ben Hogan, nor Jack Nicklaus, or Nancy Lopez. "Tiger" Woods is unique in this regard, and it is this quality that made it possible for him to excel at the highest level under tremendous stress and still succeed at such a young age. Believe me, this young man has MENSA-level strength of mind for the game of golf. And believe as well that *he learned to reach that level with mental coaching and by mental practice.*

Developing the Strong Golf Mind

So how do we learn to develop a strong mind for golf? And how do we practice? First we'll identify six key qualities that will enhance mental strength. Next, you'll be advised on how to use the Mental Practice Exercises, which are your key to creating new mental habits. There are also some "golden nuggets": observations, truths, and tips that may be just what you need to "turn on the light" and give greater insight into mental strength. Understand that there are a variety of techniques for developing strength of mind. No absolute list of characteristics can define it. But from my forty years as a teacher and player of the game, I feel the following selection will be of great value regardless of your skill level.

Six Qualities of Mental Strength

Relaxation

I often start group golf clinics with a demonstration: I stand in front of the students holding a club lightly between my thumb and forefinger, swinging it freely back and forth in a 180-degree arc. While doing so, I describe the admirable qualities of this pendulum motion—rhythm, acceleration, and consistency, all desirable elements of a good golf swing. Then as the group continues to watch this to-and-fro motion, I say that I'm about to kill the swing— "Watch!"—and it stops dead in a vertical position. My question to them is: "How did I stop it?" The correct answers come in slightly different forms but all point to the same basic cause. "You squeezed it," or "You tightened your fingers," or "By adding grip pressure," all are acceptable descriptions of how to kill a swing. They have just observed and identified the reason why so many golfers find making a consistent golf swing a difficult task. Too much squeezing, tightness, and pressure is a regular occurrence among golfers. This is unfortunate because **the greatest destroyer of a golf swing is excessive**

A pendulum can swing freely until . . .

. . . the grip is squeezed.

muscular tension. That realization is the basis for almost every mental technique on performance enhancement that is described in this book. Muscular tightness, particularly in the shoulders, arms, and hands slows speed, shortens the golf swing's arc length and width, inhibits the squaring of the clubface, and destroys rhythm and timing. Relaxation and muscular tension are mutually exclusive conditions. Knowing that should make it self-evident that *the ability to relax is one of the most valuable tools in the golfer's mental arsenal.* That is why it is the first technique listed among your Mental Practice Exercises.

Relaxation is a very learnable skill that can be accessed in a variety of ways. The form that we offer you is known as differential muscular relaxation, which is induced through imagery. The technique entails progressively working through several key muscle groups in the body and getting them to reach a more relaxed state. One of the advantages to this system is that while it requires some practice to get results, a great deal of practice is not necessary. It is recommended that you use this first technique of the Mental Practice Exercise system in the locker room or parking lot, or wherever you change your shoes prior to going to the practice range or the first tee. A very effective way to practice this relaxation technique is to put the message on a cassette tape and listen to it on a Walkman during your exercise time, or when taking a walk, riding a bike, or other quiet times. When you can induce relaxation by this method and then maintain a similar state during play, your swing performance will improve. *Keep in mind that this is a learned skill that must be practiced, not one to be pulled out only on golf competition days.*

Mental Practice Exercise #1 (for relaxation)

Locate a comfortable chair or seat and sit in your most restful position. Close your eyes, relax, and then say to yourself: "I am in a very restful place—the beach, the woods, a mountain retreat, a lovely meadow, or a cozy room on a snowy night. As I picture my special place I will start to feel more calm; calm and relaxed; relaxed over my whole body. Everything will also begin to feel like *it is slowing down.* **Then I'll focus on my hands and fingers feeling they are warm and relaxed, almost limp. . . . Now my forearms will begin to become free of tension. My biceps and shoulders will relax, feeling warm as my arms and**

To relax before play, find a comfortable space: under a tree, in a golf car, in the locker room.

hands now begin to feel heavy. . . . My neck will relax and my head will feel very heavy . . . very heavy. . . . I will feel my facial muscles relax and my jaw will feel limp. . . . Then the back of my neck and upper back muscles will gradually lose their tension. . . . Next my chest and stomach will begin to relax as my breathing becomes deeper and slower; in and out; deeper and slower. . . . A feeling of warmth will go down into my legs and buttocks. . . . My thighs, then my knees and calves will feel free of tension and very relaxed and heavy; warm and relaxed. . . . I will gradually feel all the tension flow slowly downward and drain out through my toes. . . . I feel very calm; calm and at ease; tranquil and very relaxed."

Let this exercise progress slowly, taking four to five minutes to complete. It will definitely help the rhythm on your first swing.

Additional Insights and Observations on Relaxation

The following are additional insights and observations on relaxation that show how valuable it is to playing better golf.

1. The desired mental brain wave state for performance in golf is alpha. It can be induced through several modalities, one of which is music. While playing in my first U.S.G.A. Senior Open Championship, I used a Walkman with alpha-programmed music to reach that state and relieve tension. It was very effective in helping me to make the cut.

The right music or sounds (preferably alpha rhythm) on a Walkman can keep you calm.

2. Tensing the muscles, holding the tension for a few seconds, then completely releasing is an effective on-course form of muscle relax-

ation. Give yourself enough time to refocus and create the relaxed but ready state you desire.

3. Controlled deep breathing is an age old technique for trauma reduction. *Slow, deep, but not forced, breathing on the course is an effective tension reducer.*

4. Seeing things in slower than normal motion and matching yourself to that pace can help relieve the temptation to speed up under stressful competitive conditions.

5. There are many techniques that promote relaxation in addition to those mentioned: hypnosis, autogenic training, modeling, positive self-talk, biofeedback, etc. But why not try a very simple one?—*smiling!*

6. I frequently use a technique that I've labeled "creative blindness." It is done by closing the eyes and rehearsing the stroke, particularly a putt, chip, or pitch. When you don't see the ball, a calmness comes over the swinging motion that frees the muscles from restriction. Capture that more relaxed feeling, then very slowly open your eyes, ready to repeat

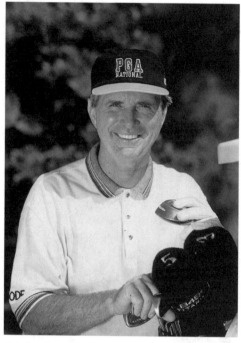

It is hard to be tense when you are smiling.

the same feeling with the ball in the swing's way.

Additionally, I would highly recommend that the reader investigate acquiring the skill of Transcendental Meditation. It takes considerable practice but produces a deep form of relaxation that is not only good for your golf but also for everyday life.

Closing your eyes on short-shot practice strokes will help you relax.

Confidence

If you really want to become a better golfer, you need to develop a high level of confidence in your abilities; it might be your single greatest mental asset when it comes to an improved game. No performer, be it pianist, actor, stand-up comic, ballerina, high-wire artist, or athlete (golfers in particular), can survive without it. *Confidence is knowing you can do something—not thinking you can— but "knowing."* The exciting news about confidence is that one does not have to be born with it. Not only *can it* be a learned trait, *it most often is.* Those who seem to be "naturally confident" may have a hereditary predisposition in that direction, but a confident attitude is still one that must be acquired. Confidence is a choice, something you can rely on even when things are not going well during a round. You can't always wait for something good to happen to be confident. If you are mentally tough, you stay confident even when the drives are missing the fairway and the putts are missing the cup.

Think of anything that you do well, a skill in which you have a high level of confidence, and ask yourself, "Where did that come from?" The answer will inevitably be the same: practice, experience,

Staying confident when your shots are missing their mark is a part of being mentally tough.

and successful performances. When you practice a skill long enough, hard enough, and correctly, you will develop a level of comfort in performing that skill that exudes confidence.

But what about performing that same skill in the competitive arena? That's where experience plays a role, because an additional psychological aspect is introduced. If the competitive circumstance is unfamiliar, the normal level of comfort may be exceeded and a subsequent deterioration in perfor-

Confidence is boosted by frequent, correct practice.

mance the result. In other words, *practice in itself isn't enough to get you ready for competition. To be successful in the heat of competition you should also include specific "game-like" practice.* The good news is that it can be as simple as simulating situations in your mind as you work on your game. Practicing a putt late on a pleasant summer evening on the green outside the golf shop and imagining that it is for your club's title, or the city publinks senior championship, or to make the cut at Tour Qualifying School, may do the trick when that actual time comes. If you make the experience real enough, when the actual moment arrives you are more comfortable and possibly even confident for having visited this scene before, albeit in your mind.

Confidence promotes trust in what you are doing. The inhibitors of a free-flowing swing, such as indecision, fear, hesitation, tentativeness, doubt, and overconcern with result, disappear with the feeling of trust. That is why you will so often hear teachers of the game saying, "Trust your swing." They know that building trust and confidence will allow you to do all that you are capable of doing.

Learn to memorize *Mental Practice Exercise #2* (page 42) as a form of self-affirmation, of instilling confidence and subsequent trust. Most important is

Be patient: A good shot can wipe out some misplays.

the closing portion of this statement, which is meant to protect you from an insidious habit to which even the best players fall victim—the negative habit of *giving up.* A few bad breaks or bad holes can discourage players enough to make them figuratively throw in the towel. Don't quit. Keep in mind that a series of good breaks can wipe away the sour taste of the previous bad streak.

Mental Practice Exercise #2 (for confidence)

"I am a good player. I am a smart player. Like a professional, I know what I can do. I don't let my fellow competitors, the course, or spectators negatively influence me and keep me from doing what I know I can do. I am tough, I don't quit, and I don't need excuses."

Additional Insights and Observations on Confidence

1. A lack of confidence can lead to these common swing wreckers: *steering,* or attempting to guide the club and consequently the shot to the target; *forcing,* or using excessive muscular involvement in the swing; *left-brain thinking,* or trying to cognitively capture mechanical details while the swing is under way.

Trying to steer or guide the ball just doesn't work.

2. Using selective memory is one mental technique to help maintain confidence. It's easy: Simply remember the good shots and forget the bad. You can't afford to hang on to baggage (bad rounds, bad shots, bad experiences) that steals your energy and undermines your confidence. So put them far on the back shelf of your brain and bring the good ones to the front. My pet term for this is "constructive amnesia."

3. "Choking" in a sport infers that the player has not lived up to his/her potential when tested in competition. It happens when the perceived stress reaches a level beyond which the performer is accustomed. The result is a loss of confidence and poor performance. The answer is to reduce the perception that the outcome is truly threatening and put it in perspective. *Nothing in golf is life threatening. GOLF IS A GAME!*

4. Dyschrony means worrying about the past or future, neither of which will help your golf. *Stay in the present* and simply make the very best shot you can at the time, then go and do it again. That's advice from the late great Bobby Jones, and it is still powerful today.

5. Think of yourself as a biological data-recording system that logs every golf shot you have ever hit. When reporting the result to your brain, put the good shots in **bold type** and the poor ones in agate type. Your shots are creating your golfing biography, and *your biography becomes your biology.*

Put the bad shots in agate type.

6.   If you want to handle pressure well and become a stress seeker (one who plays better in competition than practice) rather than a stress avoider (one who tends to collapse under pressure), *use your selective memory* to recall situations in life where you came through in "the clutch." Start thinking of yourself as "game tough" and tell yourself, "I'm good when the heat is on."

Positive Visualization and Imagery

One of the most commonly used mental tools among world-class athletes is positive visualization, or mental imagery. Springboard divers picture their moves and mentally rehearse them before stepping onto the board. Downhill ski racers review in their minds each turn and twist that must accompany their descent down the slope. Track and field athletes see themselves clearing the crossbar, sailing over the hurdles, slinging the javelin without fouling, all in perfect form prior to their event being called. Top-class golfers do the same. Do you? If you are like the vast majority of people who play this game, instead of seeing success, you frequently picture disaster: the ball being topped into the water, slicing or hooking into the woods, chili dipping into the bunker. We've all done it. Maybe the better question would be, "What is your most common picture, one of perfect precision or probable peril? If you regularly use imagery, is it negative or positive? Are the divers seeing their foot slip on their hurdle step and their bodies losing control? Do skiers picture themselves falling down, ski tips shooting sky-

Mentally picturing bad shots before you hit makes them come true.

ward, while coming out of the chute? Are high jumpers imagining missing their steps and hitting the crossbar on the way up? Definitely not! That kind of negative imagery interjects worry, adds tension to the muscles, and eventually produces precisely what was pictured; classic self-fulfilling prophecy. *So take a lesson from world class athletes: Create positive mental images if you want positive results.*

Everyone visualizes, albeit to varying degrees. Unfortunately for most golfers, negative pictures dominate positive ones. That certainly is not the case with the "superstar" players. Dr. Bob Rotella, in his fine book *Golf Is Not a Game of Perfect,* relates an encounter with Fred Couples in which he asked Fred about his mental approach to the game. Couples's response was, "I pull up my sleeves and shrug my shoulders to try to get them relaxed, and then I try to remember the best shot I ever hit in my life with whatever club I have in my hand." That, my fellow golfers, is powerful. No mechanical details, only pictures, and pictures of the highest quality.

Use *Mental Practice Exercise #3* (page 50) to stimulate a positive visualization habit. Learn to picture the shot with a particular club just the way you'd like to hit it every time. Start with putting, then imagine playing some chips and pitches while focusing on your technique and how the shot feels.

Picture yourself hitting the putt that is going to go in . . .

On all the shots, see positive results. Change clubs, then move on to full iron shots. Finish with your driver and repeat that swing six times. Let yourself sense how those good swings felt. Take the practice of positive visualization with you to the course and add it to your preparation before each shot. Like Fred Couples, picture the best shot that you have ever hit with that club. If you don't come up with a good picture, step back and start again. The best thing about this procedure is that when you get a negative picture you can always delete it and restart. Call it a "mental Mulligan." If the negative thought is strong, you will have to put yourself into your most powerful mental override mode. You may need several of the mental strength strategies that are recommended throughout this book. Caution: Don't continue your routine while harboring negative thoughts. Stop, then start all over again. Remember, *you and only you control the pictures. Don't miss the shot in your mind before you swing the club, because then it's already too late.*

Mental practice Exercise #3 (for positive visualization)

"I know what my best strokes and best swings look like and I will rehearse by picturing them. Starting on the putting green I will see myself calmly stroking putts in from 3, 6, 9,

and 12 feet, feeling a relaxed flowing motion in each stroke. I'll then visualize making some short chips and pitches, seeing the ball simply getting in the way of my measured swinging motion, which then sends it to the target. Next I will hit a few sand wedge pitches and bunker shots using a bit more body and arm

... or the perfect form for chipping.

motion. I will follow with the full iron swing, using a #9, #7, #5, #3, hitting each shot so it lands on the green. Finally, I'll finish with my driver, making six consecutive swings to a balanced finish, seeing the desired ball flight and feeling the power that comes from letting go of tension. I will now picture in my mind a tee-to-green round, seeing only positive results on the course I play next. I'll do this while relaxing, as visualization is enhanced by relaxation."

Additional Insights and Observations on Positive Visualization and Imagery

1. Using images can be tremendously powerful. In fact, *images can be as strong as the actual event*. A United States military officer imprisoned for five years in a Vietnam POW camp visualized in detail playing golf every day. After his release, he returned home and within weeks shot a 75 in a tournament. He had been an 8 handicap player before his tour of duty.

2. Star borrowing, or the *picturing of a great player* and trying to reproduce his/her action, is one form of effective visualization for peo-

ple who have reasonable skills in copying or mimicking. Children are particularly adept, but anyone can do it.

3. Have a videotape made of your swing hitting selected shots with various clubs. Choose your very best swing with each club and have it repeated on the video five to ten times. Watch the tape to fix in your mind a strong image or visual picture of your best swing. This is self-modeling, and can include putting, bunker play, chip and pitch, etc.

Watching yourself on video is a great teaching aid, particularly if it is a loop sequence of your best swing.

If you see straight down the middle every time you step on the
tee, you will hit more successful drives.

4. The primary reason players often make spectacular trouble shots, causing the ball to go under, around, and over obstacles, is that *they work harder on visualizing these shots* than on those from less demanding positions. This fact only serves to further validate the power of visualization.

5. Moe Norman, reputed to be golf's all-time straightest hitter, says when he is on the tee, "all I see is straight down the middle, straight down the middle." Wouldn't you consider that to be an advantage? Is it available to you? Yes, in your mind.

6. One of the greatest putters who played professionally was the late Labron Harris, Sr. His mechanics were plain vanilla, nothing fancy. So what was his secret? *He made every putt in his mind first before he stroked it.* That's positive visualization!

Concentration and Focus

If the average round of golf takes four hours, and a player's normal score is 90, what percentage of that time would be consumed with actually swinging the club to hit the ball? Approximately 150 seconds out of a possible 15,000 . . . or 1 percent. Add to that the preparation time before making the swing and you still have close to 13,000 seconds when you are not playing golf but walking, riding, or waiting to play. *So really, there is only a small amount of time in a round of golf that you need to concentrate.* However, focusing for a few seconds without letting outside thoughts or interference disrupt you is not easy. Try it! Look at an object in the room and let all other thoughts disappear. Do this for only thirty seconds and you will find that it is difficult to keep out flashes of thought, outside interference, or momentary wanderings. Focusing sharply is not as simple as it would seem. Therefore, trying to remain sharply focused, shutting out the outside world for four hours on the golf course, is not really possible. Focusing for a very brief period of time to prepare for and make a shot is much more feasible, but it takes practice.

There are two phases of mental focus on each golf shot. First, is the preparation phase, which Dr. Richard Coop and I called the "analytical phase" in our book *The New Golf Mind*. That's when the left side of your brain is sizing up the problem at hand and taking in information like a computer. After absorbing the available information, the brain begins analyzing it. For example: How far is it to the

It is not easy to focus on a singular object for 30 seconds without being distracted.

flagstick? What is the direction and strength of the wind? What is my ball flight tendency in these conditions? Where is the trouble? How hard is the green? Where do I stand in the competition? *It takes*

Analyze the conditions before club selection.

but a few seconds to gather this information, yet all the data needs to be used in making the decision on the type of shot and club to select.

Now the second phase of mental focus can be entered. That is the "integration," a function of the right side of the brain, which is creative rather than analytical. Details now must disappear and pictures appear. The focus is on sensing, visualizing, rehearsing, centering, settling, targeting, readying, and finally, doing. But it is a totally different mindset than its predecessor the analyzer. The integrator seeks to focus on feel rather than mechanical detail. It lets go of cognitive thought and relies on muscle memory. It seeks flow rather than position. The focus is on allowing rather than causing. *It may be the most difficult task in golf to focus on not trying to overcontrol the result, but rather to let the result just happen.*

All of this can be accomplished with your Mental Practice Exercise #4, which is a well developed preshot routine. *The great value to a preshot routine is that it not only helps you with consistency by adding precision to your preparation but also gets your focus away from result and into process.* In other words, you pay closer attention to the business at hand, the preshot routine and the visualized swing, than to what might happen to the ball once it leaves the clubface. If in selecting a recipe, say for a birthday cake, you choose to deviate from the specific ingredients used on a previous occasion, you will get a result that is not consistent with what you achieved before. It is the same in making preparations for your golf swing. A consistent preshot routine helps overcome one of the game's most difficult challenges: inconsistency. So develop a routine. It will eventually become automatic. You may not need to think about it, yet you must still put your focus on being precise in executing the elements within it. That takes discipline! Consequently, *losing focus on just a few swings per round can ruin what otherwise might have been a good score.*

Mental Practice Exercise #4 (for concentration)

"I have a routine that I follow for each shot, which brings me into focus, allowing me to concentrate on the task at hand."

- **Assess the lie, conditions, distance, and the situation.**

- **Picture the desired shot and where it will finish.**

- **Select the right club to fit the picture.**

- **Begin the preshot routine by seeing the target line and the resulting shot.**

- **Take the grip, aim the clubface, align the body, get the stance, and establish ball position.**

Reading the greens is the assessment part of putting.

- **Waggle for comfort and either visualize your shot or picture your swing again, and capture the feeling to produce the result.**

- **Swing the club while trusting the swing.**

- **Evaluate the result. If it's good, internalize it. If it is not, practice a successful effort and visualize the desired result.**

Additional Insights and Observations on Concentration and Focus

Concentration and focus are important to good performance, providing that the focus is on something that produces the desired result. Too often when the player focuses on "hitting the ball" rather than "swinging the club," the flowing motion is aborted and the finish incomplete. The tightening of muscles in an attempt to strike is so visually evident it appears as though the player were hitting a ball made of steel, or swinging into a solid brick wall. Focus on "slinging," or almost letting go, and that's when you'll feel the flow.

I encounter players who seem to regularly have a couple of bad holes in a round to spoil what otherwise would be good scores. *They consistently look for faulty swing mechanics but should more often investigate loss of focus.*

1. Many athletes in other sports seek solitude just prior to competition, focusing their mind on the upcoming performance. I've often wondered why more golfers haven't seen the need to quietly *focus their mind instead of only focusing on their mechanics during warm-up.* Us-

If you focus on slinging, you will feel the flow.

Other athletes often seek solitude before performing: Why not golfers?

ing either your Mental Practice Exercise card or a prerecorded audiotape in a Walkman can make the experience consistent no matter where you are playing.

2. In studying the greatest putters of all time I found it interesting to note where they placed their attention when putting. Once the reading and aim were completed, *none focused on mechanics; almost all focused on feel and pace.*

3. The deepest form of concentration comes when you are not thinking about trying to concentrate but rather are totally absorbed in the present.

4. The late Harvey Penick often said, "Take dead aim," which is simply another way to tell you to *focus.*

Emotional Control and Attitude

Golf offers its participants the full range of human emotion, from exhilaration after scoring a hole in one, to despair when losing by three-putting the last green from a short distance. *Our emotions have a big influence on our performance, since they possess the ability to chemically alter the body; that same body that swings the club.* Consider the biological effect of anger or fear on the body. Each can produce an elevated heart rate, rise in body temperature, increased muscle tension, a lessened ability to think rationally, and in severe cases nausea and tremors. None of these age-old limbic responses to prepare the body to fight or flee are useful in golf. Yet anger and fear are frequent companions for golfers. How

A bad lie doesn't stop a mentally tough golfer.

well we control these and other negative emotions will largely determine our resulting attitude, and attitude is one of the key components for acquiring mental strength.

We can't control the weather, our opponents, the condition of the course, good and bad breaks, and sometimes not even our shots, but we can control our attitude toward them. *Attitude is nothing more than the emotional response you make to happenings and circumstance.* When Jack Nicklaus hit a perfect drive on the closing hole of the Doral Tournament a few years back needing only a final par to be the winner, rather than being rewarded he found instead he was penalized because his ball ended up precisely in the middle of a large divot hole. What do you think was his reaction? He certainly could have gotten angry or even fearful over the possibility that this could cause him to mishit the shot and lose the tournament. Instead, he took a bit more time to survey the situation, selected his iron, fired the ball cleanly onto the green, and two-putted for the victory. After posting his score and accepting the trophy he was questioned by the press about the obvious bad break on the drive. He said, "Actually, that bad lie may have helped me since I was forced to focus on staying down through the shot." That's putting a definite positive spin on what could have been an emotional "why me" negative response. Nicklaus was in control of his emotions and his attitude.

A hotshot teenage junior golfer from Texas, later to become a PGA Tour player, was used to hitting fifteen to sixteen greens a round in regulation, shooting scores quite often in the low seventies. When he missed more than a few greens, he'd shoot much higher scores and would get visibly upset, displaying fits of anger. His home PGA professional got fed up with the young man's attitude and told him if he wanted to see a real player he should attend the Tour event in town the following week to watch two-time PGA champ Dave Stockton.

The boy did and came back amazed. He said, "That guy Stockton only hit six greens all day. I hit that in nine holes."

"Did he slam his club in the ground when he missed a green?" asked the pro.

"No," said the junior player.

"What did he shoot?" asked the pro.

"Sixty-nine," said the young man, who then added a telling comment: "And he acted like that was the way you were supposed to play!"

"Well now you have seen a real golfer," concluded the pro.

A "real golfer" can do some amazing things. The inspirational para-plegic trick-shot golfer, Dennis Walters, is a great example.

So what was the lesson? *A strong short game can take you a long way, but a great attitude is a necessary companion.*

When Seve Ballesteros was near the peak of his career he played in our PGA Championship and had two very mediocre opening rounds with a total score that appeared to be higher than the projected cut. He returned to his hotel, made hasty airline reservations for Spain, packed, checked out, loaded the car for the airport, and was ready to leave when a bellman came out and said there was a phone call for him. Tournament headquarters was calling to say that the afternoon scores had been very high and Steve had just made the cut. His tee time was 7:38 the next morning. Think of the situation. He had no realistic chance to win the tournament and was already mentally on the plane home. Yet he dutifully unpacked, checked back in, and played the final two rounds, grinding on every shot and returning scores in the sixties, which produced a respectable finish. At the same time several players of lesser reputation who also had just barely made the cut were simply going through the motions of playing with obvious disinterest, and consequently finished near the bottom of the field, not even making expenses. The difference? *Attitude*.

In all three examples attitude was critical. Nicklaus did not let an obvious bad break anger him or affect his attitude. That's mental strength! Stockton's strong self-image as a player allowed him to maintain a positive attitude despite a day of below-average ball striking. That's mental strength! Ballesteros displayed a remarkable attitude of not quitting, no matter how far back he was in the pack. That's mental strength! All three had a choice. *Attitude is always a matter of choice*. They all chose like champions. In tough circumstances, how do you choose?

Mental Practice Exercise #5 (for emotional control and attitude)

"I know that my emotional state and attitude affect my performance. I also know that I am solely in control of both. Negative emotions like anger and fear produce physiological swing destroyers. So, I will stay cool, confident, and positive. I will have a good attitude, even when things aren't going well, because it will help me play better as well as gain the respect of my peers."

Have some fun in golf: It is better for you than anger.

Additional Insights and Observations on Emotional Control and Attitude

1. Despite any previous performance you should approach each shot with the expectation of success, *desiring it but not requiring it.* That's a good golfing attitude.

2. Many people have *unrealistic* expectations of how well they should play considering how little time they invest in practice. When one

Realize before play that you will hit a few bad shots in the round; then you won't be surprised or get upset. That's realistic.

combines meager preparation with high expectations, the result can create a negative attitude toward the game, the teacher, and oneself. So get real—or at least get realistic! Small efforts produce small rewards.

3. The saying, "As a man thinketh, so shall he be," is a classic concept that has surfaced in other languages and cultures for thousands of years. What you think about life, other people, situations, conditions, and yourself is

what creates your attitude. Knowing that peers can influence our attitude may be why "old pros" suggest that you *hang around good putters because they "thinketh" positively.*

4.   What we eat or drink before or during a round can have a biochemical effect on us that influences our emotions. *Caffeine and sweets are examples of poor choices as they can lead to slight tremors and a quick physiological high followed by a sudden low that can negatively affect the emotions.*

5.   *Gain a proper perspective* when facing a situation that might cause undesirable emotional arousal. Such an occasion could arise when playing with a famous personality. In such an instance, remember, they are just people. A nurse once told me that she had attended to the rich, the poor, the famous, and the anonymous, and no matter who they were they all needed a bedpan. Not a bad image to keep things in perspective.

6.   There is at least one instance I can imagine where *anger can be useful* in golf. That is when you get so angry with your performance that you decide to practice.

If anger motivates you to practice, then it is good.

Motivation

All the good advice, talent, equipment, and opportunity in the world won't make you a better player if you aren't motivated enough to apply yourself. You need some passion for the game—the same passion that you should use to motivate yourself to practice physically, mentally, and biomechanically.

First you must decide what you want, how badly you want it, and what you are willing to do to get it. Is your desire to break 100, own a single-digit handicap, be the best man/woman/junior/senior at your course, become a professional, or to simply beat your know-all-about-it golf neighbor? In order to energize yourself beyond just wishing and into action, you need a goal, an objective, or a dream that becomes concrete. Without such a target, the fires that fuel momentary action will quickly dissipate.

Don't ever discount the power of setting goals! That process is a universally proven tool. The guidelines for goal setting are familiar to most and are quite simple. But many times "simple" does not necessarily mean "easy." The Golden Rule is one example. While the rule of "Do unto others . . . ," is simple and widely known, it is not widely followed. So it is with the motivational technique of goal setting, a valuable tool that is more talked about than practiced.

Check your goals before the practice session.

So, decide what you want from golf. Maybe it has nothing to do with score enhancement, championships, or winning matches with peers. Maybe it's about friendship, exercise, nature, travel, respite from routine, or enjoying the personal challenge. Still you have to know what you want. If not, there is a strong chance that you will get something else. If its solitude you seek then going to the course as a single at 10:00 a.m. on Saturday isn't going to meet your objective. But you must first know what that "deep down" objective is.

Once you decide what it is you want in the golf portion of your life, write down your goal or goals. Putting goals on paper enhances their empowerment. If it's an ambitious goal, say a single handicap when you are now a 23, then it must be broken into smaller minigoals and give yourself an adequate time frame to accomplish them. All goal setting should have some time limit imposed so you stay focused. The time limit can always be adjusted later, but write the completion time down along with the goals and how you plan to achieve them.

Decide what your resources are for meeting your goals. In the case of the 23 handicap player, there could be several: access to golf books and videos at the library; an excellent teaching professional at his/her home course; tournament golf on television providing good models to watch; the Golf Channel for free instruction; a local fitness center where they feature golf exercises; a store or pro shop where they sell learning and practice aids; and a new club-fitting center at the course to get the right equipment. Write those resources down, then make a plan with a weekly or monthly schedule. How much time is available? What are the practice priorities? If you have a teacher, involve him or her.

Proper clubfitting is one of the steps to meeting your goal for better golf.

Practicing with tools and learning aids gives you feedback.

Finally, post the goal or goals, maybe in several places, but at least in one that is in a prominent place that you'll see every day. I put one of my reminders on a Post-it above the door leading out from our master bathroom. It says "WARRIOR?" I know my goal. It's indelibly imprinted in my mind. And the Post-it message is cryptically saying to me, "Are you a warrior or a wimp?" Are you pursuing your goals? It's a strong reminder and a good motivator.

Use your *Mental Practice Exercise #6* (page 82), first to accomplish the goal-setting task, and then to keep yourself focused on that specific target. It's

It is harder to improve without help from a competent teacher.

quite a bit easier to get fired up than it is to stay fired up. As coaches from all sports know, *having the will to win is relatively easy, but having the will to prepare to win distinguishes the champion from the also-ran.* Without motivation, maintaining the desire to succeed is highly unlikely. What would you like to get done in your golf game? If it's better performance through greater mental strength, then use your Mental Practice Exercise program regularly.

You and your teacher should be partners in your quest for better golf.

Mental Practice Exercise #6 (for motivation)

The foundation of good performance is proper preparation. "I will decide what I want, write my goals, make a plan, and follow the plan. There may be interruptions due to sickness, travel, and unforeseen circumstances, but these are only temporary. Progress at times

**may be slow or seemingly nonexistent, but I
will persevere."***

Additional Insights and Observations on Motivation

1. *Action without a plan is unfocused wasted energy.
    A plan without action is merely a dream.* You
    need both a plan and action to stay moti-
    vated.

2. It is recommended that self-talk be kind. But
    self-criticism can sometimes be useful as a
    motivator, a wake-up call, when your focus
    has slipped and you have "gone to sleep."

3. Record keeping can be a great motivator. Re-
    member from school days the record boards
    that trumpeted the accomplishments of ear-
    lier track and field stars, swimmers, or a vari-
    ety of ball players? Those numbers pushed a
    lot of people to practice harder. Keeping your
    own stats from rounds of golf can do like-
    wise.

4. Maintaining a ringer score record at your
    home course is a motivator to *keep trying* dur-

---

*My personal golf plan is located at the end of the book.

Record keeping, like a ringer score, is just another motivational tool.

ing a round even when your game is going poorly. (A ringer score is the best number you have made for the year, or for your life, on each hole of your home course or any one that you play regularly.)

5. *Goal setting during practice sessions* can motivate you to a higher level of performance. For example, "I'm not going to leave until I make three successive putts from six feet."

Setting goals during practice, like making a certain number of putts from a given distance, will help you focus.

Selecting opponents who are more accomplished than you can *motivate you to practice* more and perform better. The choice might be either practice more or get "beat up" a lot on the course.

Finding Time Through Built-Ins

You have been given six principles for developing mental strength along with additional insights into their value and how they may be applied. But what about the time factor? Where do you find the time to play, hit balls on the practice range and do this psychological stuff too? The answer is built-ins. If you are creative and attentive you can get all that you need from the material in this book and practice it taking very little additional valuable time. Here is how.

You can get an incredible amount accomplished if you simply attach your new Mental Practice Exercises to daily routines. For example here is one way to complete all or at least some of your Mental Practice Exercises in a normal work day. Your relaxation exercise (#1) takes only three to five minutes. You could complete it around mealtimes, such as part of your lunch hour, a predinner ritual, maybe just before breakfast, or before starting your daily routine. It can always be done at the golf range prior to a practice session, but I would suggest to look instead toward incorporating it into things that you do every day. That's how to develop a good habit. Using Mental Practice Exercises #2 through #6 can all be easily tied into your daily activities. For example, your visualization skill can be done while at the sink in the morning, driving the car, riding the commuter train, doing the washing or dishes, or waiting in line at the store or bank. You can picture your golf swing and never miss a shot. Just use your imagination. Make copies of your Mental Practice Exercise card (page 95) to put anywhere you spend significant time, or carry one with you in your wallet or purse. Soon you won't need the card as you will memorize the key elements and know them by heart. Don't forget the power in the statement, "As a man thinketh, so shall he be." *Use your Mental Practice Exercise card as a constant reminder for mental strength training.*

Gary Wiren's Personal Golf Objectives

Earlier in this book we made a case for the value of goal setting in achieving objectives. I believe in its power to sustain motivation and keep you focused on what you are trying to accomplish. With that said, I offer my own personal objectives for golf. In doing so, I give appreciation to former St. Olaf, Minnesota, hockey coach Whitey Aus, who created the model for this list.

1. Set a reasonable schedule of practice and training that you can meet, and then stick to it. There will be emergencies and situations that cause an occasional miss; be as regular as possible.

2. Be positive about yourself, your game, and what you are doing. A negative attitude is one of the most destructive forces in golf.

3. Practice with an objective in mind. Since your time is short, make your practice time of the highest quality. Make each shot (excluding warm-up) as though on the course and counting for score: fewer balls; more perfect shots.

4. When playing, even in a casual round, take enough time to execute properly. As long as you are taking the time to play, even for fun, do it right. Make it a habit.

5. Winners are not always those who have finished first. A winner is someone who gives the most in preparation to reach his/her potential and makes every effort to perform at their highest level. There will be times when that is accomplished and you still aren't victorious; but you are a winner.

6. No opponent is deserving of either lack of respect or an attitude of awe. In any reasonable match of talent, either competitor can win on a given day.

7. You may not have the best talent in a match, but tough competitors often overcome superior talent. Patience and perseverance will pay off in golf.

8. Be consistent in your performance, focusing on the task at hand for the full time you are playing. Don't ease up when ahead or quit when you are behind. You never know what might happen to you or an opponent, so keep your focus. One shot at a time.

9. Self-control is a trait that you should strive to achieve. Loss of self-control is harmful to performance as well as to individual growth as a person. It reveals itself in club throwing, displays of temper, offensive language, verbal abuse of spectators or officials, complaining about the event or facility, etc. **Keep your composure!**

10. Keep your body in good physical shape by observing the following suggestions:

• Eat three balanced meals daily, avoiding as much fried foods, rich desserts, fat and salt as possible. Eat more fruits, vegetables, grains, and cereals, and get your protein. You may have heard this advice many times before, but just don't hear it, do it!

- Limit or abstain from the use of chemicals, including alcohol. Smoking is detrimental to your overall health and is out of the question.

- Get seven to eight hours of sleep a night. Fatigue destroys performance.

- Include a mixture of flexibility, cardiovascular, and strength work in your physical training program.

11. Be committed to your sport, but put competition and outcomes in perspective. There are more important things in your life than golf. Putting it in perspective will help you as a competitor to realize you don't have to win, only to give it your best effort. This attitude promotes relaxation and actually contributes to good performance.

Enjoy what you are doing. If it isn't rewarding or enjoyable, then reevaluate your program and make it so. Golf is a game and is meant to be enjoyed.

Conclusion

The reason that people take instruction is to improve. But *improvement requires change*, and change is not easy. Think of any distasteful or annoying habit that is tough to get rid of and you will know what I mean. So it is with bad golfing habits, or lack of good golfing habits, whether they be mechanical or mental. What you have just been given is a formula for greater mental strength, but it is not in itself an answer. You control the final answer which will require patience and effort. Why not go for it? Why not see how much better you could be?

To help you become the best player possible I hope you will make full use of the six keys to developing your mental golf strength that are found on the following page. You might want to remove this page from the book, place numbers 1 through 3 on one side of a 4 × 5 card and 4 through 6 on the other side, and have it laminated so that you can carry it with you for easy recall.

Note: Any references to learning or practice aid devices in this book can be fulfilled by calling Golf Around the World, 1–800–824–4279 or can be viewed at : *www.golfaroundtheworld.com*.

Mental Practice Card

1. I WILL FOLLOW MY PROGRESSIVE RELAX-ATION EXERCISE BEFORE I PLAY SO THAT I FEEL CALM AND AT EASE.

2. I AM A GOOD PLAYER AND I AM A SMART PLAYER. I KNOW WHAT I CAN DO AND WON'T LET OUTSIDE INTERFERENCE KEEP ME FROM DOING IT. I DON'T QUIT OR MAKE EXCUSES.

3. IN PREPARATION FOR AN IMPORTANT ROUND I WILL FIND A RELAXING SET-TING, THEN PICTURE THE COURSE AND THE SHOTS I PLAN TO HIT. DURING THE ROUND I WILL USE MY POSITIVE VISUAL-IZATION ABILITY TO MENTALLY SEE MY BEST SWING AND MY BEST SHOTS.

4. A DEFINITE PRE-SHOT ROUTINE WILL BE A PART OF MY PLAYING STRATEGY. IT WILL INCLUDE ASSESSING THE CONDI-TIONS, PICTURING THE SHOT, GRIP, AIM AND SET-UP, TRUSTING THE SWING AND EVALUATING THE RESULT TO EITHER IN-TERNALIZE OR REPLACE.

5. I KNOW ATTITUDE IS IMPORTANT IN IN-FLUENCING PERFORMANCE AND THAT NEGATIVE EMOTIONS ARE SWING DE-STROYERS. SO, I WILL STAY POSITIVE, EVEN WHEN THINGS AREN'T GOING WELL.

6. SUCCESS IS GREATLY DEPENDENT UPON PREPARATION. SO, I WILL WRITE GOALS, MAKE A PLAN, AND PERSEVERE.

Your Personal Mental Golf Notes